INTERNET

PASSWORD KEEPER

OWNER

PHONE NO : _____

EMAIL : _____

ADDRESS : _____

WIFI

LOCATION
(HOME, OFFICE, COFFEE SHOP ETC)

IMPORTANT WIFI
NETWORK DETAILS

Network Name

Password

LOCATION
(HOME, OFFICE, COFFEE SHOP ETC)

IMPORTANT WIFI
NETWORK DETAILS

Network Name

Password

LOCATION
(HOME, OFFICE, COFFEE SHOP ETC)

IMPORTANT WIFI
NETWORK DETAILS

Network Name

Password

LOCATION
(HOME, OFFICE, COFFEE SHOP ETC)

IMPORTANT WIFI
NETWORK DETAILS

Network Name

Password

WIFI

LOCATION
(HOME, OFFICE, COFFEE SHOP ETC)

IMPORTANT WIFI
NETWORK DETAILS

Network Name

Password

LOCATION
(HOME, OFFICE, COFFEE SHOP ETC)

IMPORTANT WIFI
NETWORK DETAILS

Network Name

Password

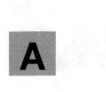

URL/ WEBSITE :

USER NAME :

EMAIL USED :

PASSWORD :   **DATE :**

SECURITY QUESTIONS :   **ANSWER :**

URL/ WEBSITE :

USER NAME :

EMAIL USED :

PASSWORD :   **DATE :**

SECURITY QUESTIONS :   **ANSWER :**

URL/ WEBSITE :

USER NAME :

EMAIL USED :

PASSWORD :   **DATE :**

SECURITY QUESTIONS :   **ANSWER :**

URL/ WEBSITE :

USER NAME :

EMAIL USED :

PASSWORD :   **DATE :**

SECURITY QUESTIONS :   **ANSWER :**

A

URL/ WEBSITE :

USER NAME :

EMAIL USED :

PASSWORD :   **DATE :**

SECURITY QUESTIONS :   **ANSWER :**

URL/ WEBSITE :

USER NAME :

EMAIL USED :

PASSWORD :   **DATE :**

SECURITY QUESTIONS :   **ANSWER :**

A

URL/ WEBSITE :

USER NAME :

EMAIL USED :

PASSWORD :   **DATE :**

SECURITY QUESTIONS :   **ANSWER :**

URL/ WEBSITE :

USER NAME :

EMAIL USED :

PASSWORD :   **DATE :**

SECURITY QUESTIONS :   **ANSWER :**

B

URL/ WEBPAGE :

USER NAME :

EMAIL USED :

PASSWORD :   **DATE :**

SECURITY QUESTIONS :   **ANSWER :**

URL/ WEBPAGE :

USER NAME :

EMAIL USED :

PASSWORD :   **DATE :**

SECURITY QUESTIONS :   **ANSWER :**

B

URL/ WEBPAGE :

USER NAME :

EMAIL USED :

PASSWORD :   **DATE :**

SECURITY QUESTIONS :   **ANSWER :**

URL/ WEBPAGE :

USER NAME :

EMAIL USED :

PASSWORD :   **DATE :**

SECURITY QUESTIONS :   **ANSWER :**

B

URL/ WEBPAGE :

USER NAME :

EMAIL USED :

PASSWORD :   **DATE :**

SECURITY QUESTIONS :   **ANSWER :**

URL/ WEBPAGE :

USER NAME :

EMAIL USED :

PASSWORD :   **DATE :**

SECURITY QUESTIONS :   **ANSWER :**

B

URL/ WEBPAGE :

USER NAME :

EMAIL USED :

PASSWORD :   **DATE :**

SECURITY QUESTIONS :   **ANSWER :**

URL/ WEBPAGE :

USER NAME :

EMAIL USED :

PASSWORD :   **DATE :**

SECURITY QUESTIONS :   **ANSWER :**

C

URL/ WEBPAGE :

USER NAME :

EMAIL USED :

PASSWORD :   **DATE :**

SECURITY QUESTIONS :   **ANSWER :**

URL/ WEBPAGE :

USER NAME :

EMAIL USED :

PASSWORD :   **DATE :**

SECURITY QUESTIONS :   **ANSWER :**

C

URL/ WEBPAGE :

USER NAME :

EMAIL USED :

PASSWORD :   **DATE :**

SECURITY QUESTIONS :   **ANSWER :**

URL/ WEBPAGE :

USER NAME :

EMAIL USED :

PASSWORD :   **DATE :**

SECURITY QUESTIONS :   **ANSWER :**

URL/ WEBPAGE :

USER NAME :

EMAIL USED :

PASSWORD :   **DATE :**

SECURITY QUESTIONS :   **ANSWER :**

URL/ WEBPAGE :

USER NAME :

EMAIL USED :

PASSWORD :   **DATE :**

SECURITY QUESTIONS :   **ANSWER :**

URL/ WEBPAGE :

USER NAME :

EMAIL USED :

PASSWORD :   **DATE :**

SECURITY QUESTIONS :   **ANSWER :**

URL/ WEBPAGE :

USER NAME :

EMAIL USED :

PASSWORD :   **DATE :**

SECURITY QUESTIONS :   **ANSWER :**

URL/ WEBPAGE :

USER NAME :

EMAIL USED :

PASSWORD :   **DATE :**

SECURITY QUESTIONS :   **ANSWER :**

URL/ WEBPAGE :

USER NAME :

EMAIL USED :

PASSWORD :   **DATE :**

SECURITY QUESTIONS :   **ANSWER :**

URL/ WEBPAGE :

USER NAME :

EMAIL USED :

PASSWORD :   **DATE :**

SECURITY QUESTIONS :   **ANSWER :**

URL/ WEBPAGE :

USER NAME :

EMAIL USED :

PASSWORD :   **DATE :**

SECURITY QUESTIONS :   **ANSWER :**

URL/ WEBPAGE :

USER NAME :

EMAIL USED :

PASSWORD :   **DATE :**

SECURITY QUESTIONS :   **ANSWER :**

URL/ WEBPAGE :

USER NAME :

EMAIL USED :

PASSWORD :   **DATE :**

SECURITY QUESTIONS :   **ANSWER :**

URL/ WEBPAGE :

USER NAME :

EMAIL USED :

PASSWORD :   **DATE :**

SECURITY QUESTIONS :   **ANSWER :**

URL/ WEBPAGE :

USER NAME :

EMAIL USED :

PASSWORD :   **DATE :**

SECURITY QUESTIONS :   **ANSWER :**

E

URL/ WEBPAGE :

USER NAME :

EMAIL USED :

PASSWORD :   **DATE :**

SECURITY QUESTIONS :   **ANSWER :**

URL/ WEBPAGE :

USER NAME :

EMAIL USED :

PASSWORD :   **DATE :**

SECURITY QUESTIONS :   **ANSWER :**

URL/ WEBPAGE :

USER NAME :

EMAIL USED :

PASSWORD :   **DATE :**

SECURITY QUESTIONS :   **ANSWER :**

URL/ WEBPAGE :

USER NAME :

EMAIL USED :

PASSWORD :   **DATE :**

SECURITY QUESTIONS :   **ANSWER :**

E

URL/ WEBPAGE :

USER NAME :

EMAIL USED :

PASSWORD :   **DATE :**

SECURITY QUESTIONS :   **ANSWER :**

URL/ WEBPAGE :

USER NAME :

EMAIL USED :

PASSWORD :   **DATE :**

SECURITY QUESTIONS :   **ANSWER :**

E

URL/ WEBPAGE :

USER NAME :

EMAIL USED :

PASSWORD :   **DATE :**

SECURITY QUESTIONS :   **ANSWER :**

URL/ WEBPAGE :

USER NAME :

EMAIL USED :

PASSWORD :   **DATE :**

SECURITY QUESTIONS :   **ANSWER :**

URL/ WEBPAGE :

USER NAME :

EMAIL USED :

PASSWORD :   **DATE :**

SECURITY QUESTIONS :   **ANSWER :**

URL/ WEBPAGE :

USER NAME :

EMAIL USED :

PASSWORD :   **DATE :**

SECURITY QUESTIONS :   **ANSWER :**

F

URL/ WEBPAGE :

USER NAME :

EMAIL USED :

PASSWORD : **DATE :**

SECURITY QUESTIONS : **ANSWER :**

URL/ WEBPAGE :

USER NAME :

EMAIL USED :

PASSWORD : **DATE :**

SECURITY QUESTIONS : **ANSWER :**

F

URL/ WEBPAGE :

USER NAME :

EMAIL USED :

PASSWORD :   **DATE :**

SECURITY QUESTIONS :   **ANSWER :**

URL/ WEBPAGE :

USER NAME :

EMAIL USED :

PASSWORD :   **DATE :**

SECURITY QUESTIONS :   **ANSWER :**

F

URL/ WEBPAGE :

USER NAME :

EMAIL USED :

PASSWORD :   **DATE :**

SECURITY QUESTIONS :   **ANSWER :**

URL/ WEBPAGE :

USER NAME :

EMAIL USED :

PASSWORD :   **DATE :**

SECURITY QUESTIONS :   **ANSWER :**

G

URL/ WEBPAGE :

USER NAME :

EMAIL USED :

PASSWORD :   **DATE :**

SECURITY QUESTIONS :   **ANSWER :**

URL/ WEBPAGE :

USER NAME :

EMAIL USED :

PASSWORD :   **DATE :**

SECURITY QUESTIONS :   **ANSWER :**

URL/ WEBPAGE :

USER NAME :

EMAIL USED :

PASSWORD :   **DATE :**

SECURITY QUESTIONS :   **ANSWER :**

URL/ WEBPAGE :

USER NAME :

EMAIL USED :

PASSWORD :   **DATE :**

SECURITY QUESTIONS :   **ANSWER :**

G

URL/ WEBPAGE : _____

USER NAME : _____

EMAIL USED : _____

PASSWORD :   **DATE :**

_____   _____

_____   _____

_____   _____

SECURITY QUESTIONS :   **ANSWER :**

_____   _____

_____   _____

_____   _____

URL/ WEBPAGE : _____

USER NAME : _____

EMAIL USED : _____

PASSWORD :   **DATE :**

_____   _____

_____   _____

_____   _____

SECURITY QUESTIONS :   **ANSWER :**

_____   _____

_____   _____

_____   _____

G

URL/ WEBPAGE :

USER NAME :

EMAIL USED :

PASSWORD :   **DATE :**

SECURITY QUESTIONS :   **ANSWER :**

URL/ WEBPAGE :

USER NAME :

EMAIL USED :

PASSWORD :   **DATE :**

SECURITY QUESTIONS :   **ANSWER :**

H

URL/ WEBPAGE :

USER NAME :

EMAIL USED :

PASSWORD :   **DATE :**

SECURITY QUESTIONS :   **ANSWER :**

URL/ WEBPAGE :

USER NAME :

EMAIL USED :

PASSWORD :   **DATE :**

SECURITY QUESTIONS :   **ANSWER :**

URL/ WEBPAGE :

USER NAME :

EMAIL USED :

PASSWORD :   **DATE :**

SECURITY QUESTIONS :   **ANSWER :**

URL/ WEBPAGE :

USER NAME :

EMAIL USED :

PASSWORD :   **DATE :**

SECURITY QUESTIONS :   **ANSWER :**

URL/ WEBPAGE :

USER NAME :

EMAIL USED :

PASSWORD : **DATE :**

SECURITY QUESTIONS : **ANSWER :**

URL/ WEBPAGE :

USER NAME :

EMAIL USED :

PASSWORD : **DATE :**

SECURITY QUESTIONS : **ANSWER :**

URL/ WEBPAGE :

USER NAME :

EMAIL USED :

PASSWORD :   **DATE :**

SECURITY QUESTIONS :   **ANSWER :**

URL/ WEBPAGE :

USER NAME :

EMAIL USED :

PASSWORD :   **DATE :**

SECURITY QUESTIONS :   **ANSWER :**

URL/ WEBPAGE :

USER NAME :

EMAIL USED :

PASSWORD :   **DATE :**

SECURITY QUESTIONS :   **ANSWER :**

URL/ WEBPAGE :

USER NAME :

EMAIL USED :

PASSWORD :   **DATE :**

SECURITY QUESTIONS :   **ANSWER :**

I

URL/ WEBPAGE :

USER NAME :

EMAIL USED :

PASSWORD :   **DATE :**

SECURITY QUESTIONS :   **ANSWER :**

URL/ WEBPAGE :

USER NAME :

EMAIL USED :

PASSWORD :   **DATE :**

SECURITY QUESTIONS :   **ANSWER :**

I

URL/ WEBPAGE :

USER NAME :

EMAIL USED :

PASSWORD :   **DATE :**

SECURITY QUESTIONS :   **ANSWER :**

URL/ WEBPAGE :

USER NAME :

EMAIL USED :

PASSWORD :   **DATE :**

SECURITY QUESTIONS :   **ANSWER :**

URL/ WEBPAGE :

USER NAME :

EMAIL USED :

PASSWORD :   **DATE :**

SECURITY QUESTIONS :   **ANSWER :**

URL/ WEBPAGE :

USER NAME :

EMAIL USED :

PASSWORD :   **DATE :**

SECURITY QUESTIONS :   **ANSWER :**

J

URL/ WEBPAGE :

USER NAME :

EMAIL USED :

PASSWORD :   **DATE :**

SECURITY QUESTIONS :   **ANSWER :**

URL/ WEBPAGE :

USER NAME :

EMAIL USED :

PASSWORD :   **DATE :**

SECURITY QUESTIONS :   **ANSWER :**

J

URL/ WEBPAGE :

USER NAME :

EMAIL USED :

PASSWORD :   **DATE :**

SECURITY QUESTIONS :   **ANSWER :**

URL/ WEBPAGE :

USER NAME :

EMAIL USED :

PASSWORD :   **DATE :**

SECURITY QUESTIONS :   **ANSWER :**

J

URL/ WEBPAGE : _____

USER NAME : _____

EMAIL USED : _____

PASSWORD : _____ DATE : _____

_____ _____

_____ _____

SECURITY QUESTIONS : _____ ANSWER : _____

_____ _____

_____ _____

_____ _____

URL/ WEBPAGE : _____

USER NAME : _____

EMAIL USED : _____

PASSWORD : _____ DATE : _____

_____ _____

_____ _____

SECURITY QUESTIONS : _____ ANSWER : _____

_____ _____

_____ _____

_____ _____

J

URL/ WEBPAGE :

USER NAME :

EMAIL USED :

PASSWORD :   **DATE :**

SECURITY QUESTIONS :   **ANSWER :**

URL/ WEBPAGE :

USER NAME :

EMAIL USED :

PASSWORD :   **DATE :**

SECURITY QUESTIONS :   **ANSWER :**

K

URL/ WEBPAGE :

USER NAME :

EMAIL USED :

PASSWORD :   **DATE :**

SECURITY QUESTIONS :   **ANSWER :**

URL/ WEBPAGE :

USER NAME :

EMAIL USED :

PASSWORD :   **DATE :**

SECURITY QUESTIONS :   **ANSWER :**

URL/ WEBPAGE :

USER NAME :

EMAIL USED :

PASSWORD :   **DATE :**

SECURITY QUESTIONS :   **ANSWER :**

URL/ WEBPAGE :

USER NAME :

EMAIL USED :

PASSWORD :   **DATE :**

SECURITY QUESTIONS :   **ANSWER :**

URL/ WEBPAGE :

USER NAME :

EMAIL USED :

PASSWORD :   **DATE :**

SECURITY QUESTIONS :   **ANSWER :**

URL/ WEBPAGE :

USER NAME :

EMAIL USED :

PASSWORD :   **DATE :**

SECURITY QUESTIONS :   **ANSWER :**

URL/ WEBPAGE :

USER NAME :

EMAIL USED :

PASSWORD :   **DATE :**

SECURITY QUESTIONS :   **ANSWER :**

URL/ WEBPAGE :

USER NAME :

EMAIL USED :

PASSWORD :   **DATE :**

SECURITY QUESTIONS :   **ANSWER :**

L

URL/ WEBPAGE :

USER NAME :

EMAIL USED :

PASSWORD :   **DATE :**

SECURITY QUESTIONS :   **ANSWER :**

URL/ WEBPAGE :

USER NAME :

EMAIL USED :

PASSWORD :   **DATE :**

SECURITY QUESTIONS :   **ANSWER :**

L

URL/ WEBPAGE :

USER NAME :

EMAIL USED :

PASSWORD :   **DATE :**

SECURITY QUESTIONS :   **ANSWER :**

URL/ WEBPAGE :

USER NAME :

EMAIL USED :

PASSWORD :   **DATE :**

SECURITY QUESTIONS :   **ANSWER :**

URL/ WEBPAGE :

USER NAME :

EMAIL USED :

PASSWORD :   **DATE :**

SECURITY QUESTIONS :   **ANSWER :**

URL/ WEBPAGE :

USER NAME :

EMAIL USED :

PASSWORD :   **DATE :**

SECURITY QUESTIONS :   **ANSWER :**

URL/ WEBPAGE :

USER NAME :

EMAIL USED :

PASSWORD :   **DATE :**

SECURITY QUESTIONS :   **ANSWER :**

URL/ WEBPAGE :

USER NAME :

EMAIL USED :

PASSWORD :   **DATE :**

SECURITY QUESTIONS :   **ANSWER :**

M

URL/ WEBPAGE : _____

USER NAME : _____

EMAIL USED : _____

PASSWORD :   **DATE :**

_____   _____

_____   _____

_____   _____

SECURITY QUESTIONS :   **ANSWER :**

_____   _____

_____   _____

_____   _____

URL/ WEBPAGE : _____

USER NAME : _____

EMAIL USED : _____

PASSWORD :   **DATE :**

_____   _____

_____   _____

_____   _____

SECURITY QUESTIONS :   **ANSWER :**

_____   _____

_____   _____

_____   _____

URL/ WEBPAGE :

USER NAME :

EMAIL USED :

PASSWORD :   **DATE :**

SECURITY QUESTIONS :   **ANSWER :**

URL/ WEBPAGE :

USER NAME :

EMAIL USED :

PASSWORD :   **DATE :**

SECURITY QUESTIONS :   **ANSWER :**

M

URL/ WEBPAGE :

USER NAME :

EMAIL USED :

PASSWORD :   **DATE :**

SECURITY QUESTIONS :   **ANSWER :**

URL/ WEBPAGE :

USER NAME :

EMAIL USED :

PASSWORD :   **DATE :**

SECURITY QUESTIONS :   **ANSWER :**

URL/ WEBPAGE :

USER NAME :

EMAIL USED :

PASSWORD :   **DATE :**

SECURITY QUESTIONS :   **ANSWER :**

URL/ WEBPAGE :

USER NAME :

EMAIL USED :

PASSWORD :   **DATE :**

SECURITY QUESTIONS :   **ANSWER :**

URL/ WEBPAGE :

USER NAME :

EMAIL USED :

PASSWORD :   **DATE :**

SECURITY QUESTIONS :   **ANSWER :**

URL/ WEBPAGE :

USER NAME :

EMAIL USED :

PASSWORD :   **DATE :**

SECURITY QUESTIONS :   **ANSWER :**

N

URL/ WEBPAGE :

USER NAME :

EMAIL USED :

PASSWORD :   **DATE :**

SECURITY QUESTIONS :   **ANSWER :**

URL/ WEBPAGE :

USER NAME :

EMAIL USED :

PASSWORD :   **DATE :**

SECURITY QUESTIONS :   **ANSWER :**

N

URL/ WEBPAGE :

USER NAME :

EMAIL USED :

PASSWORD :   **DATE :**

SECURITY QUESTIONS :   **ANSWER :**

URL/ WEBPAGE :

USER NAME :

EMAIL USED :

PASSWORD :   **DATE :**

SECURITY QUESTIONS :   **ANSWER :**

URL/ WEBPAGE :

USER NAME :

EMAIL USED :

PASSWORD :   **DATE :**

SECURITY QUESTIONS :   **ANSWER :**

URL/ WEBPAGE :

USER NAME :

EMAIL USED :

PASSWORD :   **DATE :**

SECURITY QUESTIONS :   **ANSWER :**

URL/ WEBPAGE :

USER NAME :

EMAIL USED :

PASSWORD :   **DATE :**

SECURITY QUESTIONS :   **ANSWER :**

URL/ WEBPAGE :

USER NAME :

EMAIL USED :

PASSWORD :   **DATE :**

SECURITY QUESTIONS :   **ANSWER :**

O

URL/ WEBPAGE :

USER NAME :

EMAIL USED :

PASSWORD :   **DATE :**

SECURITY QUESTIONS :   **ANSWER :**

URL/ WEBPAGE :

USER NAME :

EMAIL USED :

PASSWORD :   **DATE :**

SECURITY QUESTIONS :   **ANSWER :**

URL/ WEBPAGE :

USER NAME :

EMAIL USED :

PASSWORD :   **DATE :**

SECURITY QUESTIONS :   **ANSWER :**

URL/ WEBPAGE :

USER NAME :

EMAIL USED :

PASSWORD :   **DATE :**

SECURITY QUESTIONS :   **ANSWER :**

URL/ WEBPAGE :

USER NAME :

EMAIL USED :

PASSWORD :   **DATE :**

SECURITY QUESTIONS :   **ANSWER :**

URL/ WEBPAGE :

USER NAME :

EMAIL USED :

PASSWORD :   **DATE :**

SECURITY QUESTIONS :   **ANSWER :**

URL/ WEBPAGE :

USER NAME :

EMAIL USED :

PASSWORD :   **DATE :**

SECURITY QUESTIONS :   **ANSWER :**

URL/ WEBPAGE :

USER NAME :

EMAIL USED :

PASSWORD :   **DATE :**

SECURITY QUESTIONS :   **ANSWER :**

P

URL/ WEBPAGE :

USER NAME :

EMAIL USED :

PASSWORD :   **DATE :**

SECURITY QUESTIONS :   **ANSWER :**

URL/ WEBPAGE :

USER NAME :

EMAIL USED :

PASSWORD :   **DATE :**

SECURITY QUESTIONS :   **ANSWER :**

URL/ WEBPAGE :

USER NAME :

EMAIL USED :

PASSWORD :   **DATE :**

SECURITY QUESTIONS :   **ANSWER :**

URL/ WEBPAGE :

USER NAME :

EMAIL USED :

PASSWORD :   **DATE :**

SECURITY QUESTIONS :   **ANSWER :**

O

URL/ WEBPAGE :

USER NAME :

EMAIL USED :

PASSWORD :   **DATE :**

SECURITY QUESTIONS :   **ANSWER :**

URL/ WEBPAGE :

USER NAME :

EMAIL USED :

PASSWORD :   **DATE :**

SECURITY QUESTIONS :   **ANSWER :**

URL/ WEBPAGE :

USER NAME :

EMAIL USED :

PASSWORD :   **DATE :**

SECURITY QUESTIONS :   **ANSWER :**

URL/ WEBPAGE :

USER NAME :

EMAIL USED :

PASSWORD :   **DATE :**

SECURITY QUESTIONS :   **ANSWER :**

P

URL/ WEBPAGE :

USER NAME :

EMAIL USED :

PASSWORD :   **DATE :**

SECURITY QUESTIONS :   **ANSWER :**

URL/ WEBPAGE :

USER NAME :

EMAIL USED :

PASSWORD :   **DATE :**

SECURITY QUESTIONS :   **ANSWER :**

URL/ WEBPAGE :

USER NAME :

EMAIL USED :

PASSWORD :   **DATE :**

SECURITY QUESTIONS :   **ANSWER :**

URL/ WEBPAGE :

USER NAME :

EMAIL USED :

PASSWORD :   **DATE :**

SECURITY QUESTIONS :   **ANSWER :**

URL/ WEBPAGE :

USER NAME :

EMAIL USED :

PASSWORD :   **DATE :**

SECURITY QUESTIONS :   **ANSWER :**

URL/ WEBPAGE :

USER NAME :

EMAIL USED :

PASSWORD :   **DATE :**

SECURITY QUESTIONS :   **ANSWER :**

URL/ WEBPAGE :

USER NAME :

EMAIL USED :

PASSWORD :   **DATE :**

SECURITY QUESTIONS :   **ANSWER :**

URL/ WEBPAGE :

USER NAME :

EMAIL USED :

PASSWORD :   **DATE :**

SECURITY QUESTIONS :   **ANSWER :**

URL/ WEBPAGE :

USER NAME :

EMAIL USED :

PASSWORD :   **DATE :**

SECURITY QUESTIONS :   **ANSWER :**

URL/ WEBPAGE :

USER NAME :

EMAIL USED :

PASSWORD :   **DATE :**

SECURITY QUESTIONS :   **ANSWER :**

URL/ WEBPAGE :

USER NAME :

EMAIL USED :

PASSWORD :   **DATE :**

SECURITY QUESTIONS :   **ANSWER :**

URL/ WEBPAGE :

USER NAME :

EMAIL USED :

PASSWORD :   **DATE :**

SECURITY QUESTIONS :   **ANSWER :**

URL/ WEBPAGE :

USER NAME :

EMAIL USED :

PASSWORD :   **DATE :**

SECURITY QUESTIONS :   **ANSWER :**

URL/ WEBPAGE :

USER NAME :

EMAIL USED :

PASSWORD :   **DATE :**

SECURITY QUESTIONS :   **ANSWER :**

URL/ WEBPAGE :

USER NAME :

EMAIL USED :

PASSWORD :   DATE :

SECURITY QUESTIONS :   ANSWER :

URL/ WEBPAGE :

USER NAME :

EMAIL USED :

PASSWORD :   DATE :

SECURITY QUESTIONS :   ANSWER :

R

URL/ WEBPAGE :

USER NAME :

EMAIL USED :

PASSWORD :   **DATE :**

SECURITY QUESTIONS :   **ANSWER :**

URL/ WEBPAGE :

USER NAME :

EMAIL USED :

PASSWORD :   **DATE :**

SECURITY QUESTIONS :   **ANSWER :**

URL/ WEBPAGE :

USER NAME :

EMAIL USED :

PASSWORD :   **DATE :**

SECURITY QUESTIONS :   **ANSWER :**

URL/ WEBPAGE :

USER NAME :

EMAIL USED :

PASSWORD :   **DATE :**

SECURITY QUESTIONS :   **ANSWER :**

R

URL/ WEBPAGE :

USER NAME :

EMAIL USED :

PASSWORD :   **DATE :**

SECURITY QUESTIONS :   **ANSWER :**

URL/ WEBPAGE :

USER NAME :

EMAIL USED :

PASSWORD :   **DATE :**

SECURITY QUESTIONS :   **ANSWER :**

S

URL/ WEBPAGE :

USER NAME :

EMAIL USED :

PASSWORD :   **DATE :**

SECURITY QUESTIONS :   **ANSWER :**

URL/ WEBPAGE :

USER NAME :

EMAIL USED :

PASSWORD :   **DATE :**

SECURITY QUESTIONS :   **ANSWER :**

URL/ WEBPAGE :

USER NAME :

EMAIL USED :

PASSWORD :   **DATE :**

SECURITY QUESTIONS :   **ANSWER :**

URL/ WEBPAGE :

USER NAME :

EMAIL USED :

PASSWORD :   **DATE :**

SECURITY QUESTIONS :   **ANSWER :**

URL/ WEBPAGE :

USER NAME :

EMAIL USED :

PASSWORD :   **DATE :**

SECURITY QUESTIONS :   **ANSWER :**

URL/ WEBPAGE :

USER NAME :

EMAIL USED :

PASSWORD :   **DATE :**

SECURITY QUESTIONS :   **ANSWER :**

S

URL/ WEBPAGE :

USER NAME :

EMAIL USED :

PASSWORD : **DATE :**

SECURITY QUESTIONS : **ANSWER :**

URL/ WEBPAGE :

USER NAME :

EMAIL USED :

PASSWORD : **DATE :**

SECURITY QUESTIONS : **ANSWER :**

URL/ WEBPAGE :

USER NAME :

EMAIL USED :

PASSWORD :   **DATE :**

SECURITY QUESTIONS :   **ANSWER :**

URL/ WEBPAGE :

USER NAME :

EMAIL USED :

PASSWORD :   **DATE :**

SECURITY QUESTIONS :   **ANSWER :**

T

URL/ WEBPAGE :

USER NAME :

EMAIL USED :

PASSWORD :   **DATE :**

SECURITY QUESTIONS :   **ANSWER :**

URL/ WEBPAGE :

USER NAME :

EMAIL USED :

PASSWORD :   **DATE :**

SECURITY QUESTIONS :   **ANSWER :**

URL/ WEBPAGE :

USER NAME :

EMAIL USED :

PASSWORD :   **DATE :**

SECURITY QUESTIONS :   **ANSWER :**

URL/ WEBPAGE :

USER NAME :

EMAIL USED :

PASSWORD :   **DATE :**

SECURITY QUESTIONS :   **ANSWER :**

T

URL/ WEBPAGE :

USER NAME :

EMAIL USED :

PASSWORD :   **DATE :**

SECURITY QUESTIONS :   **ANSWER :**

URL/ WEBPAGE :

USER NAME :

EMAIL USED :

PASSWORD :   **DATE :**

SECURITY QUESTIONS :   **ANSWER :**

URL/ WEBPAGE :

USER NAME :

EMAIL USED :

PASSWORD :   **DATE :**

SECURITY QUESTIONS :   **ANSWER :**

URL/ WEBPAGE :

USER NAME :

EMAIL USED :

PASSWORD :   **DATE :**

SECURITY QUESTIONS :   **ANSWER :**

URL/ WEBPAGE :

USER NAME :

EMAIL USED :

PASSWORD :   **DATE :**

SECURITY QUESTIONS :   **ANSWER :**

URL/ WEBPAGE :

USER NAME :

EMAIL USED :

PASSWORD :   **DATE :**

SECURITY QUESTIONS :   **ANSWER :**

U

URL/ WEBPAGE : _____

USER NAME : _____

EMAIL USED : _____

PASSWORD :   **DATE :**

_____   _____

_____   _____

_____   _____

SECURITY QUESTIONS :   **ANSWER :**

_____   _____

_____   _____

_____   _____

URL/ WEBPAGE : _____

USER NAME : _____

EMAIL USED : _____

PASSWORD :   **DATE :**

_____   _____

_____   _____

SECURITY QUESTIONS :   **ANSWER :**

_____   _____

_____   _____

_____   _____

URL/ WEBPAGE :

USER NAME :

EMAIL USED :

PASSWORD :   **DATE :**

SECURITY QUESTIONS :   **ANSWER :**

URL/ WEBPAGE :

USER NAME :

EMAIL USED :

PASSWORD :   **DATE :**

SECURITY QUESTIONS :   **ANSWER :**

V

URL/ WEBPAGE :

USER NAME :

EMAIL USED :

PASSWORD :   **DATE :**

SECURITY QUESTIONS :   **ANSWER :**

URL/ WEBPAGE :

USER NAME :

EMAIL USED :

PASSWORD :   **DATE :**

SECURITY QUESTIONS :   **ANSWER :**

URL/ WEBPAGE :

USER NAME :

EMAIL USED :

PASSWORD :   **DATE :**

SECURITY QUESTIONS :   **ANSWER :**

URL/ WEBPAGE :

USER NAME :

EMAIL USED :

PASSWORD :   **DATE :**

SECURITY QUESTIONS :   **ANSWER :**

URL/ WEBPAGE :

USER NAME :

EMAIL USED :

PASSWORD :   **DATE :**

SECURITY QUESTIONS :   **ANSWER :**

URL/ WEBPAGE :

USER NAME :

EMAIL USED :

PASSWORD :   **DATE :**

SECURITY QUESTIONS :   **ANSWER :**

URL/ WEBPAGE :

USER NAME :

EMAIL USED :

PASSWORD :   **DATE :**

SECURITY QUESTIONS :   **ANSWER :**

URL/ WEBPAGE :

USER NAME :

EMAIL USED :

PASSWORD :   **DATE :**

SECURITY QUESTIONS :   **ANSWER :**

URL/ WEBPAGE :

USER NAME :

EMAIL USED :

PASSWORD :   **DATE :**

SECURITY QUESTIONS :   **ANSWER :**

URL/ WEBPAGE :

USER NAME :

EMAIL USED :

PASSWORD :   **DATE :**

SECURITY QUESTIONS :   **ANSWER :**

URL/ WEBPAGE :

USER NAME :

EMAIL USED :

PASSWORD :   **DATE :**

SECURITY QUESTIONS :   **ANSWER :**

URL/ WEBPAGE :

USER NAME :

EMAIL USED :

PASSWORD :   **DATE :**

SECURITY QUESTIONS :   **ANSWER :**

URL/ WEBPAGE :

USER NAME :

EMAIL USED :

PASSWORD :   **DATE :**

SECURITY QUESTIONS :   **ANSWER :**

URL/ WEBPAGE :

USER NAME :

EMAIL USED :

PASSWORD :   **DATE :**

SECURITY QUESTIONS :   **ANSWER :**

URL/ WEBPAGE :

USER NAME :

EMAIL USED :

PASSWORD :   **DATE :**

SECURITY QUESTIONS :   **ANSWER :**

URL/ WEBPAGE :

USER NAME :

EMAIL USED :

PASSWORD :   **DATE :**

SECURITY QUESTIONS :   **ANSWER :**

X

URL/ WEBPAGE :

USER NAME :

EMAIL USED :

PASSWORD :   **DATE :**

SECURITY QUESTIONS :   **ANSWER :**

URL/ WEBPAGE :

USER NAME :

EMAIL USED :

PASSWORD :   **DATE :**

SECURITY QUESTIONS :   **ANSWER :**

URL/ WEBPAGE :

USER NAME :

EMAIL USED :

PASSWORD :   **DATE :**

SECURITY QUESTIONS :   **ANSWER :**

URL/ WEBPAGE :

USER NAME :

EMAIL USED :

PASSWORD :   **DATE :**

SECURITY QUESTIONS :   **ANSWER :**

URL/ WEBPAGE :

USER NAME :

EMAIL USED :

PASSWORD :   **DATE :**

SECURITY QUESTIONS :   **ANSWER :**

URL/ WEBPAGE :

USER NAME :

EMAIL USED :

PASSWORD :   **DATE :**

SECURITY QUESTIONS :   **ANSWER :**

URL/ WEBPAGE :

USER NAME :

EMAIL USED :

PASSWORD :   **DATE :**

SECURITY QUESTIONS :   **ANSWER :**

URL/ WEBPAGE :

USER NAME :

EMAIL USED :

PASSWORD :   **DATE :**

SECURITY QUESTIONS :   **ANSWER :**

URL/ WEBPAGE :

USER NAME :

EMAIL USED :

PASSWORD :   **DATE :**

SECURITY QUESTIONS :   **ANSWER :**

URL/ WEBPAGE :

USER NAME :

EMAIL USED :

PASSWORD :   **DATE :**

SECURITY QUESTIONS :   **ANSWER :**

URL/ WEBPAGE :

USER NAME :

EMAIL USED :

PASSWORD :   **DATE :**

SECURITY QUESTIONS :   **ANSWER :**

URL/ WEBPAGE :

USER NAME :

EMAIL USED :

PASSWORD :   **DATE :**

SECURITY QUESTIONS :   **ANSWER :**

URL/ WEBPAGE :

USER NAME :

EMAIL USED :

PASSWORD :   **DATE :**

SECURITY QUESTIONS :   **ANSWER :**

URL/ WEBPAGE :

USER NAME :

EMAIL USED :

PASSWORD :   **DATE :**

SECURITY QUESTIONS :   **ANSWER :**

URL/ WEBPAGE :

USER NAME :

EMAIL USED :

PASSWORD :   **DATE :**

SECURITY QUESTIONS :   **ANSWER :**

URL/ WEBPAGE :

USER NAME :

EMAIL USED :

PASSWORD :   **DATE :**

SECURITY QUESTIONS :   **ANSWER :**

Z

URL/ WEBPAGE : _____

USER NAME : _____

EMAIL USED : _____

PASSWORD :   DATE :

_____   _____

_____   _____

_____   _____

SECURITY QUESTIONS :   ANSWER :

_____   _____

_____   _____

_____   _____

URL/ WEBPAGE : _____

USER NAME : _____

EMAIL USED : _____

PASSWORD :   DATE :

_____   _____

_____   _____

SECURITY QUESTIONS :   ANSWER :

_____   _____

_____   _____

_____   _____

Z

URL/ WEBPAGE :

USER NAME :

EMAIL USED :

PASSWORD :						**DATE :**

SECURITY QUESTIONS :				**ANSWER :**

URL/ WEBPAGE :

USER NAME :

EMAIL USED :

PASSWORD :						**DATE :**

SECURITY QUESTIONS :				**ANSWER :**

Z

URL/ WEBPAGE :

USER NAME :

EMAIL USED :

PASSWORD :   DATE :

SECURITY QUESTIONS :   ANSWER :

URL/ WEBPAGE :

USER NAME :

EMAIL USED :

PASSWORD :   DATE :

SECURITY QUESTIONS :   ANSWER :

Z

URL/ WEBPAGE :

USER NAME :

EMAIL USED :

PASSWORD :   **DATE :**

SECURITY QUESTIONS :   **ANSWER :**

URL/ WEBPAGE :

USER NAME :

EMAIL USED :

PASSWORD :   **DATE :**

SECURITY QUESTIONS :   **ANSWER :**

12345678

URL/ WEBPAGE : _____

USER NAME : _____

EMAIL USED : _____

PASSWORD :   **DATE :**

_____   _____

_____   _____

SECURITY QUESTIONS :   **ANSWER :**

_____   _____

_____   _____

_____   _____

✉ 📶 ✉ 📶 ✉ 📶

URL/ WEBPAGE : _____

USER NAME : _____

EMAIL USED : _____

PASSWORD :   **DATE :**

_____   _____

_____   _____

SECURITY QUESTIONS :   **ANSWER :**

_____   _____

_____   _____

_____   _____

12345678

URL/ WEBPAGE :

USER NAME :

EMAIL USED :

PASSWORD :   DATE :

_____

SECURITY QUESTIONS :   ANSWER :

URL/ WEBPAGE :

USER NAME :

EMAIL USED :

PASSWORD :   DATE :

SECURITY QUESTIONS :   ANSWER :

12345678

URL/ WEBPAGE :

USER NAME :

EMAIL USED :

PASSWORD :   DATE :

_____   _____

_____   _____

_____

SECURITY QUESTIONS :   ANSWER :

_____   _____

_____   _____

_____   _____

URL/ WEBPAGE :

USER NAME :

EMAIL USED :

PASSWORD :   DATE :

_____   _____

_____   _____

SECURITY QUESTIONS :   ANSWER :

_____   _____

_____   _____

_____   _____

URL/ WEBPAGE :

USER NAME :

EMAIL USED :

PASSWORD :   **DATE :**

SECURITY QUESTIONS :   **ANSWER :**

URL/ WEBPAGE :

USER NAME :

EMAIL USED :

PASSWORD :   **DATE :**

SECURITY QUESTIONS :   **ANSWER :**

HELPFUL INTERNET TERMS

BROWSER : The software package or mobile application that lets you view web pages, graphics, and various content. Examples of which are Chrome, Firefox, Internet Explorer, and Safari.

DOMAIN NAME : A part of an Internet address located at the right of the last dot that is used to identify the type of organization using the server, such as .gov, .com, .edu.

DOWNLOAD : To copy a data from one computer system to another via the Internet.

HOMEPAGE : Default starting page of a website, usually the contents of the site are listed on this page.

HTTP or Hypertext Transfer Protocol : The data communication standard/protocol of web pages. It is used to send and receive webpages and files on the internet.

HTTPS or Hypertext Transfer Protocol Secure : This specifies that the webpage has a secured layer of encryption added to hide your personal information and passwords from public access. This is an added feature when you log in to your online bank account or when you shop online upon enter of credit card information to look for "https" in the URL for security.

ISP or Internet Service Provider : A generic term for any communications company that can connect you directly to the Internet.

HELPFUL INTERNET TERMS

JPEG or Joint Partner experts group or Joint Photographic experts group: A file format for graphic images (Eg. photos, vectors) on the Internet.

MALWARE : These are malicious software or code, which includes any harmful code—trojans, worms, spyware, adware, etc. that were designed to collect information and sometimes would the computer system.

PASSWORD : A secret word, number, characters or combination that must be used to gain access to an online service or to modify software for a secured access of information.

PHISHING : This is an online form of fraud where someone tries to trick the victim into revealing secured information details, such as a username, password, or credit card details by masquerading as a trustworthy entity or website in electronic communication.

POST: To upload information to the Web via different website or social media.

SEARCH ENGINE : An Internet service that helps you search for information on the web. Example of which are Google, Bing, etc.

SMART TV : Any television that can be connected to the Internet to access streaming media services and can run entertainment applications such as on-demand videos access, services, Internet music and Web browsers.

HELPFUL INTERNET TERMS

SMS or "SHORT MESSAGE SERVICE" : a form of text messaging on mobile phones, sometimes used between computers and cell phones.

SOCIAL MEDIA : Online communities or social networks, where people share information like photos, music and personal views etc. There are many social networking websites e.g. Twitter, LinkedIn, Snapchat, Pinterest, Instagram, Facebook.

SOFTWARE : A program, or set of instructions, or documentation of procedure that runs on a computer. This includes applications and operating systems.

SPAM : These are unsolicited e-mail, or junk mail. Most spam is either a bunch of marketing ads, financial scam, gaming or sexual in nature. Internet service

SPYWARE : Softwares accidentally or pushed installed on individual's computer, which collects information of the user without their knowledge or consent and sends it back to the creator of the spyware program. It tracks the computer's use and create numerous pop-up ads. Most spyware can damage the entire computer system and facilitate identity theft.

SURFING : This activity involves users browsing around various websites following whatever interests them.

HELPFUL INTERNET TERMS

URL or Uniform Resource Locator : Address of a site on the internet. For example, the URL for the YouTube is: www.youtube.com Each URL is unique.

UPLOAD: To send information from your computer to another computer via internet.

USERNAME : The name a user selects to be identified on a computer, on a network, social media or gaming forum.

VIRUS : A malicious software program loaded onto a user's computer without the user's knowledge. These viruses performs self-replicating program that typically arrives through e-mail attachments and which multiplies on the hard drive, quickly exhausting the computer's memory and worst destroys all operating system. Trojan is a classic example of a computer virus.

WORLD WIDE WEB (www or web): A hypertext-based navigation system on the Internet that lets you browse through a variety of online resources, using typed commands or clicking on assorted links for information in words, graphics, videos etc.

IMPORTANT NOTES :